Mother Octopus

Sarah Giragosian

Mother Octopus
©Sarah Giragosian, 2024

Books may be purchased in quantity and/or special sales by contacting the publisher. All inquiries related to such matters should be addressed to:

Middle Creek Publishing & Audio
9161 Pueblo Mountain Park Road
Beulah, CO 81023
editor@middlecreekpublishing.com
(719) 369-9050

First Paperback Edition, 2024
ISBN: 978-1-957483-21-4
Cover Art: DALL-E AI Image of Octopus, edited and altered.
Cover Design: David Anthony Martin, Middle Creek Publishing & Audio
Author Image: Elise Bouhet

Mother Octopus

Sarah Giragosian

Middle Creek Publishing & Audio
Beulah, CO   USA

In memory of my mother,
Carol Vienneau

Table of Contents

III.   Foreign Bodies

"She's lost among the spaces/ inside letters, moth light, moth wind,/ a crumpled poem in place of love."

—Reginald Shepherd, "How People Disappear"

I.   In the World of Sham and Nought

Saltonstall Residency, Ithaca, NY Haibun

Underwater once: all you now ogle. Breakneck falls and scattershot strawberries, chirring spring peepers and toss of the dice black-and-white warblers, caroming from branch to branch. Gorges aplenty. If you slacken your pace, the rocks will recite their not-so-secret histories. If you hike their glacier-grinded faces, you might backtrack to the long centuries of glacier-melt and the birth of rivers bursting forth, their apprentice tides hammering land into shape, making room for the rawboned deer that samples the compost at dusk and wild hollyhock that ornaments the trail behind the artists' studios. Dub each wild strawberry an injunction, its sweet flame a reminder to savor the summer. Mind the plunk of caterpillars raining from the trees; someday they'll snuff out your breath as American Ladies. Mind the blind man caning forth his own path, but don't stare at his bandaged head, fresh blood smeared at the edges. Mind the artist pottering around until dinnertime or her next vision: crows trailing a red tail hawk like a breakaway skirt. Or grief still glinting in the dead artist's bedroom like a precious bell, too tiny to lose. Outside, the cows are braying from faraway.

> A mother's vast tongue
> licks her calf into being,
> flush with a new idea.

In the World of Sham and Nought,

the children forgot the names
        of the feral creatures first.

They didn't know enough
        to miss the engrossment of fur

or notice the oil-iridescence
        in puddles that necklaced

once the grackle's gloss.
        They had no sense of nest,

no armor inspired
        by carapace, no flock

of notes in their mouths
        to right the skies back

to birdsong or humming gods.
        Here is the beehive,

Where are the bees?
        Hidden away where no one sees.

Their imaginations inbred,
        they lost the scent, then the names:

a jaguar's a car,
        a red bull's a brand,

and cartoons have nothing to do
        with the scatter of stiff wings,

the aftershock of hooves
        in a pen. And there will be time

to press your ear
        to the earth when you're dead.

No whimper, no downcast deer.
        No *gooseflesh,* only *hair*

on end. No more memories
        of elephants, price tags on their heads.

Lost Girls

In my dream, *L* is gone: loop, light, lemon and all the words that include the letter L have been culled from the alphabet, erased. Or perhaps they never existed or were recanted or— like a pair of gloves—were simply mislaid (it's hard to know the field of logic, the barriers of the possible, in a dreamworld), and I find myself in a place where no one remembers or speaks the words that include the letter. Imagine: the dominion of *L* exiled from consciousness. Leaf, blood, lungs, waterlilies: these tongue-to-palate exertions, these down-to-earth nouns no longer flow from my mouth. Imagine the children reciting *h-i-j-k-m-n-o-p*. Imagine the elision, the elles lost. Elles ont disparu. The girls, I wish to tell you, are missing. But neither my mother tongue nor your adopted one (our common one) converges any longer. Imagine trying to say, *I love you* in an alphabet that has never conceived of love or of wildness, swaddle, pull, or pillow. No leaves trembling above. No lull of the lullaby in the nursery. No longing. No ebullience. An austere dictionary.

How do I say that I'm writing you a love letter? In phonology, *L*, if pronounced before a vowel, is light, but after, dark. Say lamp. Say fell. Bereft again of the letter that I could hardly pronounce as a child (*Mary has a yittle yamb,* I would sing in full-throated trochees), I could not even explain my lisp to you, my *L*'s plundered from my language in my parallel dreamworld. The bull's eye of a word well-selected in the right order: that satisfaction, I worried, I might never feel again. What a strange aquarium of a world-inside-a-world that I float in. *L*'s on my lips, but out comes bubbles. And you, Elise, are a different person, I feel, a woman living inside the perimeter of a 25 letter alphabet.

Welcome to America,

where the children play
cage to cage.
    We've taken back our country,
my countrymen say from the sunny side
of empire, while mothers in airtight cages do time,
their babies playing mercy in nurseries lined
with steel bars, each day their captors
ho-humming away their nine-to-fives.

    And when the president,
in another televised scolding
into the sequined air says,
Over the border, they're sending explosives!
he means *missives,* but it's all the same
to him, and they are all
      the same to him.

Some configurations of my mother tongue,
cage that it is, bring such shame.
The myths become muscle memory,
but any Land of the Free,
any opportunity with a deadbolt
is a head game.
    Immigrant, you know the game's
rigged, and the bullets on your bones
were never meant to be even,
and the state will have its way
with your body.

Immigrant: hide away your hope
    with its bubble sheen in your lunch tray,
      store your soul behind the pellet-
        hard peas, for safekeeping.

I'm afraid to map my heart
in these badlands, this sad land
where they say I *belong*, meaning

at its root
             to go along with. Let me not

                   belong, if this is belonging.

Snowy Owl Nocturne

The earth is burning, the glaciers are calving,
but for now at least (though all is melting) I'm an echo

of snow, a belonging. So many secrets I tuck into my feathers—
the particular skies, for instance, that saddle me home

each spring. If you can, look through the frozen well,
I'll be the match of flame below. I read and I read

the book of night. Some winters
I stay and every page, every day is darkness

without horizon or shadow. I am that stillness,
wind-blasted day upon daylong night, feathers riffling,

a rockface against Arctic wind. If you should spy a white blot
interrupting the icescape—an ice blink?—

look for me. Consider what white-outs I've witnessed,
my forehead pressed like a satellite against the abyss.

Breaking through the Chernobyl Exclusion Zone

"Unprotected Russian Soldiers Disturbed Radioactive Dust in Chernobyl's 'Red Forest', Workers Say"

—Reuters, March 29, 2022

No glowing eyes, no fifth limb,
but the gray wolves of Chernobyl,
free for a time of humanity, nip and kill,
lope and roam—thrive, their numbers swelling
seven times their normal size, and maybe
there will be time for the pines to rally back,
though when the liquidators spotted them spitting
up rust-red leaves, fuel for radioactive fires,
they bulldozed them back.
Earth to earth, ash trees to ashes.
Dead, they could go on forever;
all these years with fewer fungi and insects,
they've hardly decayed.
    Child, it's too late
for butterflies and rebirth, but here's
another cracked planet, another cracked bell jar.
Can you set the story straight?
Can you remember how in the fairy tales,
even the darkest ones, when the soldiers
stationed in the enchanted forest discovered a curse
had settled into their cells, it had a name
other than collateral damage, and *ashes to ashes,*
dust to dust inflected an elemental goodbye?

    Once upon a time—
but how to tell this story?
    How to stake out lyrical territories
for nuclear fallout
     and wolves our most fatal
       creations cannot contain?
Once upon a time, dust meant dust
 and rain meant rain,

and the ravens, once loyal to wolves,
          flew every which way, forgetting the landscape
had been magicked into a vault.
And all the birds in the Exclusion Zone,
     smaller brained, dwindled,
          particularly females, overstrained by reproduction.
Lonely, all the males sing
          and sing, awful,
               awful in their doubled volume.

Open Country, Open Road

Chip away at the clichés of the American road trip—
the youthful, hair-in-the-wind abandon or the cross-country
imbroglios of the nuclear family—and what's left?

The backseat scenery: the boom and bust lands,
the industrial work lights swallowing the highways,
the pumpjacks nipping the prairie like grotesque bobbleheads

leering across amber waves of grain. The road unrolls
ahead like film strip slipped from its projector
and in the dead air, a jilted crow plays tug of war

with a deer hock jackknifed on the highway.
On our way to discover our country,
we air piano to the sounds of another pastoral dream

on the radio. As for me, call me jaded,
call me the nagging reminder of carbon emissions,
the kid-in-the-back who won't shut up,

who hasn't discovered yet that all the parents,
2.5 siblings, and dog are all rolling their eyes
at me, this outlier of anxiety who would trade all the spoils

of empire for fewer than yearly hundred-year floods.
Oh say can you see the Milky Way? No, no matter;
all of it's lost to LED lights anyway.

Seeking out the tonic of wilderness? The jig's up.
Our roadway games have all played out:
I spy sore eyes, I spy kleptocrats, I spy toxic flares

from Canada to Nigeria where kids pay for Shell's pipedreams,
and in the blear of nightmare, I'm singing through the smog.
And when I catch myself seeking a land unlooted,

I try to re-route us: no more wrong turns towards Arcadia.
No more do-gooder dreams dressed in racism.
Can you see the signs? *Trespassers will be shot,*

the trees tell us, or maybe they're ghosts,
overcompensating. They remind us that even the wild,
full of ears, is half-invented thing.

Thumbnails of America

America, do you ever stop and wonder,
                How did this become my life?
Do you ever ask why you haven't aged
                out of your cornflake tastes,
your flipbook sentiments, your gun to head
                demands? Do you wish for a heart
less like a turnstile or a mother tongue
                other than a dollar? You're a hustler,
a crowd pleaser, a lover of security
                gate rituals. I feel you screening
my face, patting me down
                with your eyes when I return to you.
Today, lonely, you're jonesing for scapegoats
                but Sunday you'll devote
to polishing trophies or strong-arming history.
                You don your equipment, God and suspicion,
offhandedly, but what do you wear
                under your skirts? Ghosts—so many—the net
effect of centuries of collateral damage.
                And in your pocket, what are you fingering?
Could be crackerjacks,
                could be a trigger. No matter.
I know this though: you made me,
                then creased me down the middle
with your greasy thumb.
                We are that fold, that divided part.

OCD

To survive this exile, you will need
to hold court with the moon, store the memory
of its light in a mason jar for later.
Understand: there's no field guide for this,
for what you will encounter, for when the sluice
gate of your mind opens, for the whetstone
of your doubts or the homespun loop of *Whys?*
Even when your mind seems to have nothing left
to plunder, *What if,* in a certain key,
snags at your heart again. If you could dare
the feral child of time to stop cuffing your wrist
to drag you down another detour, you might
just make it, but you can't let go.

To survive this exile, plan for the times
your thoughts will turn to snapping turtles;
it's safest to approach from behind. Beware the tail,
the backlash and tango of open possibilities.
Keep close the sprig of secrets that grow
just below your chest pocket. You'll need poetry
to face this, and metaphors like blinkering flashlights
to pass among your people if you return.

Migration Story

We move because we must.
Because war, famine, rising seas.
Because sometimes the ruins
ask you to leave them be
and sometimes they settle inside you.
Because we're a species
that trusts in the calculus of improbable dreams.
Because the land's heating up, and like coyote,
we'll tail the scut of the rabbit through the burning leaves.
Because our exodus out of Africa is a songline
inscribed in our DNA, and our allegiance to wind
has outlasted any territory, any terrors
inside of it.
                    Sculling through the sea,
I feel the nick of history underneath
my sneakers; can you? Can you sense
the saltwater splashing into the hull
comes from the source?
                    Because you and I will
need to wager on what grows beyond our porch,
and like the pulsing moons of jellyfish
or lambent scatter of monarchs,
we'll submit to a future thrust.
Because if you go,
I will follow. Fold in your wings, friend;
rest awhile. Your blood still flows.
Because the body's provenance
is the first crossed boundary.

Field Guide for the White Naturalist
or: The Trees Speak a History I Did Not Know

Instructions with a Disclaimer: If you bring this guide into the field, keep in mind that it is best read with a wariness of white spaces, identifications, and curations. Carry a pen and a pair of scissors; you may have to fill it in and undercut its whiteness as you read. Do not trust what you think you know.

~~Lapdog (canis)~~

    Description: known to runaway slaves as a bloodhound or savage dog; a tracker of skin oils & cells; trained to fight until the death; slaves traveled through muddy water or wore rabbit grease on their feet to throw the dogs off their scent

        what did the dogs know?

                what omissions

            what skins

what odor of terror & rabbit,

                what curse

    what coercion

Migrating birds (migratus)

    Description: a cue for flying north; a summoning

      what does it mean to take flight

          your heart   *a bird*

     smacking

        against your rib cage.

        When from the sky,

            a sign

Oak Tree (quercus)

Description-America's ~~national~~ tree; ~~wholesome and~~ strong, likes full sun; in the night: a hanging tree

to set out in the night

Ocean (oceanus)

Description-a middle place; a passage; "there was hardly room…some went mad of thirst and tore their flesh/ and sucked the blood…"

With such thirst

Pine (pinus)

Description-a medicine used by slaves; an antiseptic; "Fer de lil' chilluns and babies [grannies] would take and chew up pine needles and den spit it in lil' chilluns mouths and make dem swallow"

babies & grannies

Riverbank (ripam fluminis)

Description: a road north; as in salvation

followed   the river

Sage (Salvia officinalis)

Description- a medicine used by slaves; a balm for fever and chills; antioxidant; taste: bitter, earthy; from the Latin word "salvare," meaning to be saved

saved themselves

Salt (Salis)

Description: a preserver; a corroder; as in seawater, a body of water

preserved

their bodies

Stars (Stellae)

Description: an escape map; as in follow the gourd, go underground, seek out the call of the "owl"

sought out

a voice

from the dead calm

A hoot

a beckoning

Can you trust with your life

a who

in a moonless wood?

First Cousins

Who paid for my dreams? For my five-speed jaunts
around the neighborhood, baseball cards clothespinned
to the spokes.   Click, click, click.

Never the click of a trigger, never the vicious hiss
of a racist name. Never *Kiss me goodbye before you go.*
Never needed a *just in case.*

Just the same cul-de-sacs of American grief:
la belle indifference of empire, that sick unanimal
with cowbell, grandstander ringing us to order

until we forget we are animal and as plural
as banyan roots. See it burying the bodies below
each garden variety footpath, figuring itself actuary?

Calculus of spin-doctor, death-gripper of habitat,
planter in absentia of minefields and charred merry-go-rounds
in cities of ruin.   It's left the gas on again

and set the house on fire. Strongarmed history
and hoarded its mirrors.   Ever wondered why it replaced coal
with oil? Coal strikes grind production to a halt;

pipelines keep time with empire. How did we get here?
What live wires flowed through my dog-
paddle dreams, your fishbowl delusions? As for me,

I baby-feasted on deranged dreams. Complied
with the suburban-injunction to look both ways (but saw so little),
to memorize my speaking lines and state capitals,

history's downplayed abuses.   Step on a crack,
break your mother's back, and though I moonlighted
at night choosing my angle of attack,

school taught me not to see the fault
lines on my own street. Never had to master the same set of rules
as my Black cousins. Never had a notion of the ghosts

that spoke through us when we played. And my cousins paid,
wrangling with the loopholes of whiteness,
its blinkered consciousness, even in their earliest days.

While You Were Out Message

I learned to cultivate a scowl the spring
my sixth-grade baseball coach told me to smile.

Smile! Meanwhile, joy turned up
as a front seat ride through the car wash

or a trespass through the cemetery,
where every step spawned an upleaping of frogs.

In those years of glitter nail polish and patchouli,
I survived on deli meats and logs of cookie dough,

but Emily's brother hanged himself at sixteen.
After his funeral, our folks got us burgers at McDonald's.

For fun, we made ourselves black out in her basement
after basketball practice. *Girl down. Girl down.*

Girls face-down on the yellow carpet
like a chain of daisies. And when we woke,

back to basketball practice. *Box out!* that adult refrain
still a battle cry in our ears. Back then, people wrote letters,

and at the town pool the adult swim lasted hours,
and when it ended, we baited our moms

with dead man's float galore. Era of swim caps
and scorched rainforests, botched macarena moves

no one could take back. Behind-the-bleachers
kids, we thrived on the schadenfreude

of the popular girls' studied ennui,
our geography teacher's unzipped fly.

At our loneliest, we cried in the bathroom stalls,
experimented with graffiti to mark ourselves present

or tried again to die. On the weekends,
our dads, newly single, jumped at the chance

to buy us jumbo popcorn at the movies. We OD'ed
on Robitussin, cut our braces on caramel apples,

carried quarters in our bags to call our moms
or dads from the pay phone on the days

we got stranded. We kept messages, all of them,
on a pink pad hardly anyone remembered to check.

Mother Octopus

Much is made of the final months of a mother octopus.
Dandle the lacy funk of a hundred or so serried eggs

on your arms for fifty-three months while wasting away
and *National Geographic* is guaranteed to have a field day.

Wed motherhood to martyrdom like mimic octopus
to damselfish disguise and anything less is pap.

But if you remove her optic (pituitary) glands,
she'll give up fasting, abandon her eggs, hunt and feed again.

Survive. Which is to say so much of mothering
boils down to hormones in the end. Which is to say surgery

can bend her unyielding essence. All this to say your self-sacrifices
and post-curfew headaches, line-in-the-sand declarations

stem from chemical messengers you can't see or hear
inside of you. All this to say you never had to lose

yourself for me. I wish we could clear some space,
start fresh, share a few cocktails over dinner.

We would have had so much in common: me, a paradox
in flesh, just another entry in a book of baby names

and friend to you. Here's to you, Mother,
flourishing, freed, afloat with possibility.

The Berlin Specimen

"In 1877, another specimen was discovered...known as the 'Berlin Specimen' ...the finest and most complete of all known Archaeopteryx fossils. It has been described as 'the most important natural history specimen in existence' because it so clearly demonstrates the evolutionary connection between dinosaurs and birds."
—panel at the Museum of the Earth, Ithaca, NY

If there's a saint of transitional species,
let me thank that dinosaur of miracles

for this limened beauty, forever moored
in rock, a bouquet of bones delicate as a magpie's

but weaponized. Let this fossil be an icon of the in-
between, an ancient proof of the seam between

earth and sky filigreed with three-fingered claws
and bony tail, jawed with hypodermic-needle teeth

and wings like an angel's. In the fount
of my mother's belly, my body became a doubled-

over song, arpeggio of our origins: gill-
slitted, tailed, practically finned, as fluvial

as any other being. If we come into the world as such
and a fossil is a door to another world,

how can we not wish to emulate forever
the ripple in the rock that helixes into an other?

Star-Struck

          I think God intended it for me—
the meteorite, I mean, my brush with unlikelier-
than-lottery luck. A holy terror, like a piano
tumbling from the heavens to take out some
poor creature below. Maybe God's one punchline

          is violence. That night, the living
room was so still. I remember the stillness.
Then, out of the blue, a smell—like firecrackers—
then a whoosh, and the out-of-the-blue shock
of rock hurtling through the ceiling and hammering

          through the plaster, smacking
against my radio, boring into my hip.
Worse than a stray bullet. No one can fathom it,
the pain and blaze of a shooting star.
Hotter than blue blazes. It weighs on me still.

          No one can fathom
the finger of God, his iron-hot brand. But I can.
Like Doubting Thomas, the doctor fingered
the bruise, star-struck. Tender to the touch,
that shiner was smudged into me for months:

          a whole galaxy of black and blue.
After it struck, from all over creation,
caravans of scientists and reporters
and long-forgotten friends beat down the door
to see me. They stomped all over the yard, past

          the dogwood and sweetgum,
ducked under the laundry line to greet me.
My Wonder Bread days were over. Goodbye
house. Hello stage. What a headache.
Before we broke up for good,

my husband gobbled
it up like Moon pies, all my limelight that spilled
over on him. But I never asked to shine.
I kept that meteorite for a good while,
cherished what should have killed me.

It wore me straight out,
all that fuss. In the end, more curse
than lucky break. When I ran out of cash,
I sold it to the museum for twenty-five bucks.
I still see God's face when I look up

into space, but I reckon that like the word *love*,
all it adds up to in the end is chaos.

Aphasia of Butterflies

This is the hour of the brutal present.
Consider the terror of a butterfly
who no longer recognizes herself as caterpillar.
As if the syntax of the world is reassembled over-
night, and the body—after a dark interlude—
shivers awake and shapeshifts.
What is she doing with wings?
She flies and is lucid as a jolt.
What does she have if not discovery, two weeks
or less, and all her brilliant defenses gone?

II. Salt Lick

Vacation in Lyon

Wobbly, wilting under a virus,
     I flounder under *Je suis,*
               but can't summon the rest.
I clutch at words like pick up sticks:
     Mauvais? Mal? Malade?
               At home I've left behind a fleet
of vitamins and my mother tongue,
     but you, my heart, translate.
               The pharmacy pitches all around me.
I catch you say *insomnia.* Insomnia?
     No—*somnolent*, meaning *drowsy.*
               Somnolent: a poetic word,
a marble in the mouth,
     like so much of French that I garble
               on the cusp of—
Comment dit-on? I circle the language like a bee
     looking for entry. Fluent in three,
               you manage to collect the right pills,
and again I think how easily
     my country reproduced, in various degrees,
               its varieties of ignorance in me.
(*Is it mono?* I ask Elise
     to ask the pharmacist.
               Maybe. It's hard to say, he says
in perfect English). I count out a single dose,
     and later, touring (I'm flush with resolve
               to find some pleasure here), I count the colors
in your words: ten—dix— shades
     of melon, champagne, citron,
               bright tonics for my pain.
Still, Love, I crave the nuances of you
     that I miss, being bound by English.
               Tell me: how much of your finesse,
your Eliseness, escapes me?
     An impossible question, though I know of the contagion
               in our everyday argot:

yes—bisous, mon amour.
Oui to vin and cheeseburgers. So much of you
on my tongue, so much beyond reach.

Lago de Tenno, Trentino, Italy Haibun

    As for medicinal waters, kick back at the lake where Alpine mountains saw up the sky. Small fry, like you, this lake was born from a landslide, a stroke of luck, long, long ago. Imagine all that falling to pieces over you. Here, cannon-ball and otter-ripple to your heart's content in waters turquoised by forested peaks above and bone-white rocks below. Exquisite, this shade of green-blue. This optic echo of forest and stone. This watery gemstone color you'll never see again unless you purloin it, stuff it in your pocket for darker times ahead. But already they're here: locals say that this oasis is shriveling up, and you hear a new word: megadrought, like *great thirst* but harder on your ears. Already it's un-islanded a heap of rock, underwater once, where you sloughed off your towels, unthinking. Thinking *Beach day!* before you knew the truth. This is not your legacy, you want to say, but it is. Like ballads and wrecking balls, prisons and patented seeds, trap doors and crossword puzzles. As Auden said, raindance, raindance while you can. Lap up this consolation of color while the trout zag around the mini maze

> of your legs, their backs
> winking yellow-silver in
> the high summer sun.

Salt Lick

You're my salt lick, and sometimes a white tail
hedging the dawn, and always a wild child,
standstill and spellbound in the forest,
translating blue-green moss and fern hair mood.
You're my snag at the heart, my cave of secrets,
and in the grotto the still, still pool. You're my season
of strawberries, my sun-bathing dreams.
You're that bolt of heat lightning, that flash within me.
You're a record of me, and I of you,
but in the years before the law let us marry,
we needed no proof. No stamp of approval.
And try as they did to part and reprove
us with DOMA, to tame our love with ICE,
we're the ecosystem that outlasts their cages;
we're the exchanges between wind,
sea, and air. The fossils of your tears
crystalized inside me somewhere
after all those years of salt and waiting.

Discipline

How does a world—dream or otherwise—lose a letter? How does it slip away, like spilling loose change down a well? But somehow this question is an afterthought. There's no tug of reason in dreaming.

Chiseled into Greek, Lambda signifies *L* and has a value of 30. I'm 35 this year and throughout my early childhood years, my parents and a language therapist drilled *la, la, la*— the flick and fold, the lilt and trill of it— into me. I knew but could not bend my tongue around the flection of it, though my ears thrummed with it every day. Low. Light. Owl. Even *la* has a whip in it. Like the undulation of le serpent bound by its slide-pushing, sidewinding, rectilinear locomotion, and lateral undulation. We are all of us full of our own devices.

The baby-toothed version of me did not miss L, but my parents and teachers coaxed it forth. At their urgings, I rehearsed the letter in my mind with my tongue and jaw until I could say it from the cave of my mouth, lifting my tongue from the top of my palate to plunge it to the back of my front teeth in one fluid motion. Climbing vine, crook of the elbow, flay of the tongue: *L* eventually lived inside me. Discipline a muscle day after day, and though your travails may humiliate you, after some years, a world may open.

L Word

And what would be our lingua franca in a land where lesbians are invisible but volcanic? Imagine dormant, sleepless us, even the laughter locked in our throats.

No wilderness of your hair on my pillow. No eyelash curling on your cheek. No tendrils of your legs or bloom of lilac in your pocket. No hairline crack between love and longing or labyrinth of your body to lose my way in.

Can a language sicken? Can its privation ail a person? And how do I grieve a sudden lacuna in language all by myself? So much gone, the second life of expressing ourselves again through language. Consider a life with no lesbians, only gays. And if there is no name for us, would the law let us be? To not exist in the eye of the law, we could live out no official story but our own. Let go the line of your balloon and it will find its own way.

Still, no one left on land or sea would see us, apparitional lesbians not even imagined in language. I can begin to tally the costs, remembering the lost letter, but you, my love, cannot. To not know the letter of our love, can you even count the imaginations like fallow acres laid to waste? You can long after a letter the way you long for a body, I try to say to you, but *letter*— of course— is lost. One more attempt at speech is just another knotted meaning I cannot untangle for you. And if a letter can slip away without fanfare, without mourning, what about love?

Duplex for Winter

—after Jericho Brown

Our love grew out of season: ripe fruit in fall.
What pulp we could save, we stored in jars.

> We stored in jars what we could save.
> By winter, we craved their stoppered glow.

Winter offered us nothing but craving.
Craving, we discovered, can offset barren

> ground; it's the bend out of depression
> that can ground love, bear its future demands.

We withstood its myths, false bearings,
and stand-in stories to save ourselves from fall-

> ing. This origin story's the resource
> we fall on when our failings own us or love

comes too late. Provisions we have in full.
Our love grew out of season: ripe fruit in fall.

Marriage as Hide and Seek

I am the abandoned house.
You: the seeker. Before you,
was I ever more than a lurch in the stair,
a stove needing elbow grease,
gall in the splintered bed frame?
Call off the realtors, the house flippers
and vandals. The loosestrife chokes
the backyard, and through the cracks, an undertow
of dragonflies come and go.
Some ricochet against the walls, peter out
and leave behind concentrations
of iridescent wings in the sills.
I am and am not here, hiding,
which is to say I'm shadow-
boxing loneliness again.

I am the abandoned house.
You: the seeker in the window
peeking in, daring me to declare
myself found. Count to one hundred again,
this time louder. If you could be
the shaft of light, the wedge in the door,
I could grow bold,
and when it's your turn to hide,
bear in mind this vow:
you will always be within ear-
shot of love, it's patient count,
whenever I'm around.

Hunger:

more than the first ache.
Even in this alternate galaxy
of an aviary where you hide, jilted bride
of twilight, little peregrine,
you scout out the velocity of light
in the hollow of your bones.

I hold your gold eye and I know that look,
that terror of being with yourself,
grounded.

     Captive with your tattered feathers
and your missing wing (a phantom wing?),
a torment of a twin, you ricochet
against the walls, an echo of yourself.

     What time is it, Mr. Wolf?
Time again for escape:
     when I approach, looming,
the old instinct rises in you
         like an overrun creek spilling
over a ledge. And each time you rise
your fall shocks you; the wound
reopens, and the terror
     of being a shipwreck flickers
        across your whole being.

Your mind is three times as fast
     as mine, and in it you take off,
rummage through the clouds,
        snatching lesser gods from the sky.

Hunger: a paradigm of violence.
Costly are your drives.
Costly the tethers that strongarm
you back to earth

and still the elemental singing
(the counterforce of prison)
in your bones for sky.

Taughannock Falls Haibun

Here, the theater of bird-shadows against cliff face, with its infinite joints and fractures, heightens the catharsis of waterfall. In this former sea, a stratigrapher's dream, turkey vultures play ring around the rosie with my body, while a crow riffs off the echoes of his caws against the gorge. I pause in this caesura in earth, while from the watchtower of slick rock, hundreds of feet above, an agile bird—a peregrine? No, here they were wiped out with DDT—contemplates her next nose-dive. Maybe a hawk? Sate your wanderlust and call your mother, she kak kak kaks; it's been weeks. Translate this lithic extravagance, this pre-rain scent and kettle warm-slag. If you're brave enough, work in the memento mori of your species, the fumes and plastics, that will be read in the strata by some future race. Mention too the love letter that is tucked into the same nook where vultures split their time with sky. Breathe in pine and brush up against deep time; swoon under their spell. And take note of the once-nomadic ribbon waving from a crack in a spinal cord column of limestone. When a breeze knocks loose a spark

> shower of rocks, watch
> how red cedars cling on for dear life
> in the nick of time.

As for my Mother, So for my Heart

"My mother was not a copper mine, my heart was not a sieve."
—Anne Waldman

My mother was an unearthed coin,
　　　　　my heart was not her knock-on-wood.

My mother was a blaze in the oven,
　　　　　my heart was not yeast in the bread.

My mother was a songbird,
　　　　　my heart was not an uncracked seed.

My mother was a broken windshield,
　　　　　my heart was an explosion of feathers.

Self-Portrait as Barred Owl

When you stopped breathing,
I pushed off the dock
of my life and left all the goods
for the crows. I faceplanted into brick-

heavy depths, dragged the floodwaters
of my tears for some kind of sign
of the woman who raised me
to believe in miracles

of spring salamanders under frosted
boulders and pocket-sized forests
of moss and fungi in campfire beer bottles.
When you stopped breathing,

I shriveled to a shadow (yours?),
then an owl, meaning my face
curled into a jumbo-
ear. My fingers: the clenched X

of talons. My thoughts: switchblades.
When you stopped breathing,
I disinherited all your defend-the-nest
instincts, waited for more kitchen knives

to fall from the sky. I stormed, made camp
beneath glints of steel. Begged for your call.
Whatever outpost you're on, whatever outer
limit, cry or call; I'll be ready, poised

over the backwoods of my grief,
the hitch of my ongoingness.
Nudge me with your song or signal,
the song of your signal (*who-who-who*

cooks for you?), or out of place sound—
scattershot chitters or whistle calculated to reach me.
Grief is a vigil of earth and atmosphere,
and the closest to heaven is upending

boulders and bottles. Stricken
into silence, your daughter to the end,
I'm listening, testing the lengths
of your love again.

Dark Mood Poem

Mourning is mumbling the same words
over and over: *ImissherImissherImissher,*

the origin of the word *misery,*
a word that has squandered its music,

that is *the* word. The only word.
If you could see what I do behind my eyelids,

you would need mind tricks too,
rituals of babble and cocktails incognito

to hide your thirsts. But it's trickier
than you might think to wander off

an entire zip code of sadness. One
is always being found.

And there's no *away from it all*;
even the dead, from their coffins,

are always in conference, grace on their side,
while the living fail to mention the splintered edges

of hope or go mum when your mother dies.
Death stitches them up like doll-lips or dredges up

cliches like skipping rocks stir up scum
across a pond: *Life goes on; you'll move on,*

except the one you want to go on with
is busy, underwater, at the other end.

Whale Fall

After the aftershock on the ocean floor,
      after the windfall of whale fall,
rattail fish & stone crabs, hagfish
         & bristleworms snag a place
at the banquet & tuck in to thickets
      of flesh, sloughing off bits
         and binging on the belly
           until—defleshed— the bones attract
        bone-devourers, zombie worms
           that suck & scour
the balustrade of rib cage to brightness.

        This is how I'd like to go:
as a landscape cracked open,
      or a city sprawling with feeders, the bulk of all
my history trimmed down
            to nutrient-rich meat.

I won't be a ghost, another cover-up
      for the economies of death,
       but the crux of matter:
a threshold to power for another.

        Mouthfuls of me in everybody,

    I could be any body.

Missing Person

I didn't ask to learn benevolence
towards my enemies. I said teach me

to be a blade. And I'll teach you
about being female. Let me tell you

about being tracked—
how he twitches, leans in, imbues

an entire climate around you.
How on some days, you feel his eyes

in the middle-distance clasp onto you —
or think you do, and soon

you understand you could slip through
the fingers of the world if he wished you to.

He makes sure you know
he's seen you at the bus stop,

the laundromat and grocery.
You aspire to fade into the fray,

to be the fish thrown back, to practice
until perfect a perfect ordinariness

that could deter him one more day.
You study the art of keepaway,

learn to stay just out of reach,
make your nights into foxholes.

A cop says he can arrest
if your stalker acts, but waiting is acting

and so is staging and settling in
for a woman's undoing.

Let me tell you about being female,
about the rage pent up in a folded blade,

an almost imperceptible itch
between sock and shoe.

Promenade à Deux

Courtship in scorpions is usually divided into four distinct behavioral stages...
initiation, promenade à deux, sperm transfer and separation.

—Ross LK, "Notes and Observations on Courtship and Mating"
in *Tityus (Atreus) Magnimanus* Pocock, 1897

Sometimes the wound dehisces
again to speak, which is to say I've tangoed
with scorpions before. How do I solve
the riddle of scorpion, his juddering dance?
Of pincer and sting, sidewind kiss, and venom
enough to dope the mind when I resist?

Sometimes the wound dehisces
again, tugging out ramifying stories inside
that slide in and out of focus
as cold choreography:

> the one who
> manhandled my broken hand/ the one who
> groped me on the subway/ the one who
> chased me down the library stairs—

Sometimes the wound dehisces
again to speak, unstitching my mouth.
All that foreboding and belated resistance,
the skittering retreat.

That in the geographies of my body,
I still remember the out-of-the-blue crush of them:

> the one who
> bore down on me in his pickup/ the one who
> stalked me in the last years of grad school/
> and the wound

dehisces again. In the kingdom of scorpions,
no softness can last. No serum to right my body back.

Pain Bias

"[A] Swedish study, published in 2014, found women waited longer than men to see a doctor in a hospital emergency department. This bias is amplified when it comes to reproductive health."
                    —Lydia Smith, *"Is Women's Pain Taken Seriously?"*

How is your pain?
                    When you answer, beware the god
trick-eye. Don't say cresting. Don't say eleven.

Build a papier-mache of your uterus
        and play arsonist or slasher
and scissor it to shreds.

When they say, *Don't cry,*
            plant a field of cattails
        waving for water in a homemade diorama of the Sahara.

When they say, *Hysterical,*
        do not bury your voice.
            Say each world dissolves into the next
through the sticky amber-slur
        of the maple syrup they serve on Styrofoam pancakes.
Wax lyrical in your pajamas
            about seventeenth century Dutch vanitas paintings
and all they got right:
                the skull and burning incense,
                        the tumbling wine glass.

When they won't believe your symptoms
            and slap on the wrong diagnosis again,
scatter seeds in the whorls of their ears.

Ask them if they can hear the whirring of first growth.

Dancing with Myself

Like Billy Idol, when I say I'm dancing with myself,
      I suspect what I really mean is watch me
            tempting joy. Can a girl's pleasure

ever be entirely her own?
      Ask Medusa or Hillary Clinton.
            If you're game for making space

for yourself, you must also be prepared
      to be another's monster. You can't escape patriarchy's
            event horizon, its pomp or dumb dead air.

But tuck your knife into your skirt
      and pass the liquor, and on those nights your body
            responds to music and some species

of spectacle, you'll still be in some way apart,
      dancing your way out. Exit ways marked.
            Sparks will fly. Fuck healing crystals, Medusa said,

and concreted those who looked upon her.
      Hilary rock, papered, scissored her way to the top
            and lost. Me? When I say I'm dancing with myself,

I mean is there such a thing as female abandon?
      Is it one eye closed? Two? I drink deeper
            and grow hollow as a squint of light.

Don't Be Fooled

by my beauty.
From the Flower Hat Jelly,
         I've learned   to flaunt
         my stingers,   to float
crown-like through black
waters, to be   a mouthful
      of killer ghost.   From the hair jelly,
    I've learned to be more   than frills;
I've crammed   and learned how to inflict
pain and panic in an instant,   to protect
        under the drifting islands
        of my tentacled lobes medusa-
fish and harvestfish,   prowfish and shrimp.
I've studied, and the blue
     blaze and throb of me is cut
     from the ocean—equal part flourish,
equal part crypt.   I'm the ache
of place,   the keeper
      of weaker bodies,
      the salt   in the wound.

Destroyer of Worlds

Just like me to search
for something named Destroyer of Worlds.
Killer of coral, she rises
from the seafloor and writhes
with ravenous arms of toxic spines.

Just like me to sweettalk a star-
fish, to embrace an envoy of brine
and hunger. And so much hunger——
a plague of need: enough to feast
on a reef, to be a terror of absorption.

Just like me to praise the rites of starfish
whose ardor is obscene but god-sent.
O Destroyer of Worlds, Star of Thorns,
your desire could be my own
in a marginally darker universe.

Diet and Feeding Behavior of the Hagfish, Practicing Witch of the Sea

I've heard it said that hagfish, with her love
      of dying flesh, can enter wounded whales
and fish, and feast from inside out. Above
      the ground, I've heard it said that this entails

slime, gross amounts of it, and hunger huge
      enough to scare away her rivals. Rue
the day I realized that it was too late
      to flee. Already hurt, I bit the bait;

I flit too close again. This time: a flash,
      a chokehold, slime, and me, her meat. Best to stay
away. But she—evolved to dine and dash—
      is all-devouring. When you pull away,

you'll have to play dead. She needs to feel you slack-
en. Your calm will be your counterattack.

III. Foreign Bodies

Rock Scramble Haibun

Le canyon des gueulards (The Canyon of the Yellers)

To scramble: to clamber over rocks with one's hands, to muscle up and across the floor of this crevasse with hands splayed and scraped by rubble. Welcome blisters. Welcome jagged bedrock. For days we'll keep these memories of grit etched in our hands. Still we go beetling through canyon rooms, while above, half-locked in rocks, roots the height of giraffes stretch, naked, their lives tangled up with deep time, a time my mind tries and tries to plumb. I fail and reach for metaphor, a scale I can work with. I'm not in a pocket of time, but in the maw of a wooly mammoth, flinty and sloth-like in her coat of algae that is really the bright shine of Spanish moss knitting the trees above.

Meanwhile, you— conscious of echoes and the silence astonishment commands— point out a cave, not yelling, but whispering, *Our new home,* and I can picture us going domestic in this tiny seat of primal time, nesting together in the limestone and clay, turning the ledges and rhythms of water-writing into bookshelves, painting with ochre all the animals, historic and forthcoming, on the walls, and spooning spider-style in our archive-abode, sixteen legs caught up in each other while we read stonework and fossil: giant's calligraphy that says former falls, curves that say erstwhile rapids, and in between bird trill and crag, the finer, inscrutable scribbles of love.

> A body of stone
> marries another body.
> Down she lays her roots.

Cavern Noctuary

—after Jennie Xie's "Alike, Yet Not Quite"

Underground, no sun or nuclear meltdown but a bunker
      eaten out by rainwater acid.

Stalactites cling overhead, waxworks of starched buckram,
      datum of earth time.

A chandelier of anglerfish teeth,
      tiny needles cut from rock above.

Figments of bats drape in shadows,
      their wings criss-crossed like miniature pharaohs.

Inside the earth's throat, milky-white
      flowstone ripples the walls like stirred cream.

A sudden baptism: thimblefuls
      of cavewater kiss my cheeks.

Gift of Ammonite

I lose my way again in a chamber
       of ammonite, fossilized helix, a blink
           of an eye in time that dizzies my mind back
      to an ancient seabed, to eons of embedment, heat,
and pressure, to this casting of carbonized spiral

in my palm. Every crenulation, every coil
       an excursion into earth's memory. Listen:
           if you dip your ear to the bend
      of the ocean floor, you can hear the earth humming.
If you tilt this whorl of stone to the whorl

of your ear, you can hear evolution's queer refrains,
       its tweaks and adjustments scaled to the frequency
           of tadpole shrimp, jellyfish, nautilus, and dreams.
      Listen for ruptures in time signature.
Wait the way you waited for her love to arrive.

Foreign Bodies

—inspired by the Chevalier Jackson Collection at the Mütter Museum

Swallow the bait. Face this cabinet of curiosities,
  of freak accidents, the whatnots of disaster—
    inedibles ingested by toddlers
& pica patients: hairpins & chestnuts,
  tacks & buckles, bottle caps & tooth roots,

keys & doll eyes. Guts & grimace.
  Imagine the labyrinth
     of airway and foodway, the alleyways
& cul-de-sacs of pharynx & larynx,
  trachea & lungs, all the ways the swallow

can land you in a tangle of trouble.
  Don't forget the vocational hazards
    of magicians & sword swallowers,
the safety-pin-lipped distractions
  of mothers, the stowage spaces

of toddler mouths & all the pins
  & knickknacks, brooches & backtalk,
    trinkets & whistles a preschooler can blend
into her being. These trinkets sing. Take this object;
  turn it to subject. Incorporate this craving.

Careful though of windpipe; don't let it go
  down the wrong pipe. Pass the water.
    Pass the scope & forceps.
And hold tight to your penny; there are copper and flora
  aplenty in you already.

Ornithology 103

We came to study the seagulls.
       When our field trip to the sea
              didn't pan out (budget cuts), we caravanned

to the dump, fording through oceans
       of crud to see the gulls in their habitat.
              Necklaced with binoculars, we monitored

their behavior, scribbled field notes.
       It's true: they've learned to slam and shatter
              tinned fish like clams against the rocks

and comb through swells of metals,
       denuded Christmas trees, tables protruding
              like pectoral fins, and even drowning mannequins

for stray crumbs, dabs of meat,
       and—best of all—deshelled crabmeat.
              When our professor, spying a herring gull,

wandered off, we ditched our binoculars
       and played king of the trash heap,
              rapiering freshmen with umbrellas. Too late

we turned when the gulls
       unburied the creature, when it coughed up
              bright ribbons of plastics globbed

with blood; when it shimmied on a belly
       bloated by improbable hungers towards us;
              when it dressed itself with fruit peels,

a hooked fish, a garnish of glass,
       and even its own intestines, a map
              looping back to us. Too late

I turned when it curled
      eel-slick against me
            as if I were its father.

Feathersick

"The sight of a feather in a peacock's tail, whenever I gaze at it, makes me sick!"
        —Charles Darwin

What to do (in theory) with those afterthought
      feathers, those overstuffed feathers? Peacock or Beauty,
natural selection can't touch you

          with your excesses, your thicket of unseeing eyes,
      your tail upright as a spine. Maybe it's true:
your train's costly, you're an evolutionary spendthrift,

and Darwin hated you, but maybe you,
      with colors decanted from a sun-rinsed stream,
needn't prove any code or theory. You, yoked to light,

          with galaxies of feathers swishing,
     beckon, mirage of an iridescent god.
              Imago of delight. A whiplash of desire.

A booty call more perfect
     for being undiluted by human mastery
or reason. O extra and preposterous bird, continue to rupture

     our neatest laws, stay a shock of blues, and someday—
           stumped and overcome—
     maybe we can learn to be beautiful too.

Baby Season

—a term wildlife rehabilitators use for the spring

Spring: season of squirrelfall
      and false starts. Nesting bunnies
            at the edge of thawing yards,

fledglings spilling from trees
      like wind-caught fruits.
            Over the phone, I tell you

to watch the babies from afar.
      They may not be abandoned.
            The mother may be nearby, watching,

waiting for you to leave. But you want "to help,"
      to redeem yourself for tossing out a trio
            of squirrel pups while cleaning the eaves.

You shot photographs of the scene,
      texted them to me as proof. A scrawl of fur,
            cement. In close up: eyes opened,

jaws clamped. No visible wounds.
      Give them room, an exit! I text.
            The mother will save them.

She's around, just at the edge
      of things. My thumbs are cocked guns.
            I need to believe in vigilant mothers.

Phonics for Grief

When my mother died, an owl came to teach me
the language of the night. Poor student,
I groped on the fringes of understanding,
like trying to predict where lightning
will strike from an astral map.
All night, all day, I carry my mother on my back,
a spider ferrying her hatchlings around town.
I send my loved ones grab bags
of miniature horses mid-gallop,
vanishing creatures tangible and still.
On the question of mental health, I wander
off, send out a search party to find myself.
I make topiaries of contortionist hearts,
dizzy my brain across each final memory's
tight rope walk. But I'm always plucking
the wrong strings, and though my tragedy's ordinary,
it's true: the choreography of the earth's orbit
has gone off script. Like jiggling a housekey
at my door to discover a new lock.
Engage in the same idle talk. Come apart.
Put a Do Not Disturb sign on my heart.
Yes, my mother taught me my alphabet,
but how could she have known
that all words are shadows
that barely touch all I have lost?
The owl visits, brings flashcards,
but the words don't fit between periods!
She sings out syllables, grows clawsy
with my face when I forget.

Fowl at Large

What honing dial set awry
or false hunch or storm of the century

drives the accidental bird
or dreaming poem to surface?

As for me, I had disavowed hope's
candle-to-egg devotions, spike-heeled the idea

of someday. Speaking of chicks, newbies,
and baby tortoises, if you sentence

a beehive to a bell jar, those hourglass
bees will one day spill like lava

over every lip and crevice. I swear,
I've seen those little torpedoes of joy and sting

meet and greet every goldenrod,
every marigold from here to long

after cocktail hour. Like a cacophony
of cats, so many I's without apology,

screaming their heads off,
I've lost all sense of grace,

thank god. My thirst is deeper;
it shrieks for that kite slicing through unseen

geographies, lost, windstorm-dazed,
her compass needle wild as a roulette wheel.

Self-Portrait as Tomb Raider

Underground, I'm hunting for you
      through the superstructure of your tomb,
            every false burial chamber or dead end

another snarled hope, a stitch in a web
      contrived to confuse and craze trespassers
            like me. But I can't keep away. I'll be a thief

of death for you. It's the same in my dreams:
      dusted in gypsum, damp with sweat, I'm burning
            like a torch, tunneling through. I'm combing

through offerings stockpiled for the ever-
      after: pots of beer and food, canopic jars
            brimful of viscera, jewels carved

into tigers and jackals, antelopes and falcons,
      creatures set off with real bones
            and teeth or beaded with emeralds, pearls.

Am I getting warmer? Here—a scent of ointment
      and palm wine in the air: I'm on fire now.
            When I find you deathmasked, body contracted,

wound in ancient prayers and linens,
      you're sumptuous still, even as a pressed flower,
            a chiasmus between fettered bird bones

and reverie. What gods would pass
      on this? What priests cut out your heart
            to wrap it up like a gift and tuck

it away again, just so, in the birdcage
      of your ribs? Listen, I've crossed the Nile,
            slogged through a thousand dreams,

a thousand ravines, to steal you
        back from eternity; what's left to lose now?
                If I peel back your integument, pluck out

the amulets like tiny love letters tucked
        into your bandages, can I magic you
                back to mammal, brush away at your matted

hair, slap your cheeks back to a healthy glow?
        What hell awaits those who break into
                a house of eternity? Not enough

to memorize the poem of your body
        not meant for me, not enough to let the finis
                in the cocoon be. But nothing expires

here: not you, not grief. I've busted through.
        I've come to you brazen; I've come to you broken;
                I've come to you to belt out the stammering

of my heart. What to do but bind you, a harvest of bones,
        to my back, believing in your perpetual nascence the way
                a snake's faith is stitched to her ever-shedding skin?

Little Edie on Surviving Isolation

A Cento for a Pandemic
—*For Sarah Whipple*

It's all a question of who you want to stay with.
  One needs a house to die in—
    a beautiful house!

Mother will die and I'll have to find another Libra
  to live with. Isn't it terrible mother
    isn't a man? Of course, I'm mad

about animals, but raccoons and cats
  become a little bit boring after awhile.
    I don't know. Everybody wants a raccoon

nowadays—the most tame, loving animals.
  Of course, everything's in the attic.
    Everything from sloths, otters, badgers,

chipmunks. Aren't we lucky? The hand of God
  struck at the right time. Thank *God.*
    But that's our one link to reality

in here. I play all the time. You have to do
  the same thing every day. We're breathing
    through a mask most of the time.

You have to have a lot of kimonos,
  a lot of costume changes. If I had the money,
    I'd redecorate every single room.

Virgil the Vulture Contemplates Life

That itch on your back?
Secondaries, growing back.
Exalt in the ruff of feathers, tar-black,

bristling at the nape of your neck.
Relish the ambrosia-waft
of carcass in early rot. Hiss, grunt, or sneeze,

you know how to clear a room, how to faux
seize, how to split my sides
with your hunchbacked prance.

You're a glider of thermals,
an undertaker with a taste for innards,
a gourmand affluent in gizzards,

a digester of tiny bones, cholera,
and mouse fur. And when you're done,
you, genius of bricolage, make daisy chains

from the remains: ugly duckling bits,
tails, mandibles of mice, skeins of pelage.
If I get in the way, I can count on the acid bath

of your defensive vomit
to burn more than acid rain.
Spitfire, you're more than a prowler

or meddler; with leftovers, you're sober
and your ways, though bloody,
are never profligate. A moocher?

Maybe, but better than that,
you're imbued with dinosaur-suave
each time you cock your head

to give me the side-eyes,
fold your wings in like a tent
and feed with the flies.

Daintily do you disembowel
a rat, do you dab at flecks of meat.
After flatfooting around on the frayed

ropes of your feet, you rest and nibble
at your feathers, greasy with preen oil.
A little spoiled perhaps, but rotten, no.

O Virgil, I catch you taking stock of me now and then,
but you can see I'm not ready, although it's a blessing
I suppose to know that you'd never let me go to waste.

When the Family No Longer Speaks of Their Dead

The only virtue of taboo is *bear,*
          meaning *the brown one,* whispered slantwise
to circumvent its true name.

          What's a taboo but a tradition
in silence? Your name I hardly hear
          anymore. Except the O

of it, like oxygen whistling out of the hole
          in the astronaut's space suit. I plant
that blue seed in my throat. Say *blue*

          for *broken, seed* for *defiance.*
It shoots out, unbidden, thorns and all,
          out of nowhere: when I'm parallel

parking, cutting to the right,
          sobbing. When I'm buying a gas station
cookie, dollar bills slipping from my pocket, sobbing.

          If it's true and language is not a window,
but a shadow, and you are a shadow in a shadow,
          the silhouette of a tree at night,

how do I summon you? Pare down
          the cosmos to its unutterable foreseen,
and while I know we—most of us—

          won't be even a tremble
of ink in its postscript, you will
          always be my collapsing center.

On Metaphor as (De-)Composition

Metaphor is always misbehaving.
      Call the body a measure,
           and it becomes a vessel too small for grief.

      Are you with me?

      Call grief a vessel broken on a lonely sea,
           and at its epicenter: what-ifs, blooms of *I should haves.*

Let's call the bird staggering along the beach
         heartache. Call the heartache
            Crow, bent over, gagging on a bone.

And, get this: the bone's twitching,
       a stutter of life. Then, at closer range,
          the bone's a mouse, meaning a creature bleeding out.

Note Crow nibbling the mouse, the mouse's odd twitching.
              Rodenticide?
                 Raid sprayed across some yard?

Call Crow's bloodstream a river spoiled.

But what if Crow turns away, flies treeward,
         before she, both blood and river,
                 spoils?

Let's call the mouse cached,
      left for later in the crook of an ash tree.
            See it? Then think of the tree at the edge
               of Crow's mind. Think of it fading.
                  Call the cache
                     a lapse in corvid memory.
                        Call each saved.

Then call the lapse
      a letter of invitation to bluebottle flies.

And the flies are a summoning,
        a spawning of larvae.
Call the larvae maggots,
          an entire melee,
                necrophages and pharmacies unto themselves.

Call the pharmacies the body's
        questions, in the end, and final words,
       all pinwheeling, growing, thrashing, and squirming forth.

              They are—after all— bacteria and viruses
              feasting and butterfly kissing and killing,
              all cross-stitched together somehow.

Call the cross-stitching no consolation,
              but by the merciless grace
              of that web I pass on.

Pneumothorax

Buried by a spell of pain—
cockleburs caught on my lips,
lungs brittle glass—
I called without words
for spadefuls of air.
Unearth me, said the imperative
of my spine, curling into itself.
If speaking pain is an act
of translation, I'll speak with my eyes—
words need breath.

Here: this polished stone, a memory
of turbulence. Moths eaten away
to tatters by the snap of the screen door.
I remember pain's solipsism:
the choke of it, and time like quick-
sand beneath me. If the photographer's
unspoken desire is to be seen,
I hungered for a fascination
of ravens, the fizz of their black
wings in the rain filling me up
from the ambulance window.

Tunnel of Silence

Usually associated with a passing raptor… the tunnel of silence indicates the recent flight path of a predator…Birds remain hidden, unsure where the danger is; they slowly come out of hiding over time or if a bird they trust begins to sing nearby.

—John Young and Tiffany Morgan, *Animal Tracking Basics*

And though the racket of life's suspended—
corvids riveted, linnets silenced— still
this frenzy in the brain
like a handful of hornets
resumes: *What is this trick?*
                        Is it zeroing in?
      Can it hear my pulse,
          my overloud thinking?
      Careful now: *not a twitch or flinch,*
not a word of consolation,
and in our throats' collective snags
we are one scream away
from blowing this trial of waiting.
And you should know by now
that I've felt in my soul a surveillance
colder than any raptor eye
and though this tunnel of silence
in this corridor of hemlocks
is just one tiny edge of the world,
we jailbirds, like overstretched violin strings,
are the tension that wants to make music again.

A Small Violence

The cat, out of love, killed a bird
and cached it in the house for us.
Later, I found a feather shivering near
the radiator, another pinioned in the seam
of your sweater. I imagine us in a year
or two preparing to move, the house spitting
up bones in a forgotten corner. Love,
do you remember when we crossed
that foreign river and you warned me about vipers
roiling in the icy waters? Remember the dry spell,
the low waters, the craquelure of clay
between each river pass? A forked tongue,
it led us back to a cliff side, its spine
cracked by a cascade too powerful for us
to swim under. We flatfooted penguin-wise
around the slippery rocks until we discovered
a turquoise pool; not rent apart by the fall's
frigid spray, not without a flinch,
we were pinned together by it.

Hallelujah

Do birds dreaming midflight ever rouse themselves into a world with an unfamiliar sky and an equivocal view? Shocked by an uncanny topography, how do they stay aloft in those moments? Or is it just humans that pick apart the seams between dreaming and waking? And what ineffable creatures ruffle the edges of my dreams? What tagalong animals—if not birds—would lead me out?

At the first splinter of morning light, from the cave of your mouth flies a song: *Hello love.* The words pool and lap at my mind, and I can hear an echo in my ear of some vestigial syllable tugging me into consciousness from sleep.

On waking, *L* appears like manna. Part of our mutual lexicon again, it has been restored to the language. *I love you,* I say again and again, and you wonder at my exuberance. I locate us on the same map. We share the same longitude and latitude once again. Clasped together through the same long, luminous morning hours, we laugh, we laze, and make love in disheveled sheets, and I can sing your name again. *Elise,* I say; you're all liquid in my mouth.

Do I Move You?

—on watching Nina Simone sing and dance on YouTube

Are you loose now? The arch of her back speaks, her core—
and with each inhale, each exhale, Nina's body testifies.
They never meant for us to survive, she knows and defies

them with each breath, and when she starts to sing,
the whole world goes dark, and across the expanse—
the state lines and radio frequencies, the migration routes

and no fly zones, the burning eyelash-arcs
of dying stars against the atmosphere and the deep, deep sea,
where the ethereal and monstrous phosphoresce and maunder,

her voice carries and catches. It pours acid and scrubs
steel wool against the hearts of her enemies, and it slices open,
like the sweetest fruit, the ones they bruised, the ones

who for four hundred years have lost their skin in a game
loaded against them. And when she sings, she is an entire climate,
and I am in love. That shiver in the spaces of your body,

that frisson you feel? The nocturnal birds know it too,
know it in every unforeseen updraft of air
that miracles their two-pound bird bones aloft.

The Release

Tossed up like a handful of confetti,
she, red tail, is elbowed off
like a bride to the wild, but she reels
and staggers, flies low,
a tumult of wings daring height.
Quiver-flight, girdle of light
flight, anxious-flight, flight of reckoning,
of three-month rehabilitation.
She'd been deemed release-ready,
but I wonder what landmines
in her mind have settled, which are exploding now?
We hope the late spring
sun will hail her, beckon her back
to sky, that she'll remember
this park where we found her, wounded,
and return to fluent flier
again, but for all we know, the sun's
dazzle could be a knife-
point to her eyes, and the out-
of-the-blue freedom
another kind of extraction.
Perhaps the world shivers, flusters her
in its sudden sharpness. The last time
you wandered off a subway
onto the streets of a foreign city, what signs
did you fail to follow?
A familiar maple might be an anchor
for a moment, but soon jays arrive,
strafing and screaming at her
and she has forgotten her own powers—
counterpoint of attack, swift beak
to belly. Maybe only higher gods
can mend trauma's corrosions
of the mind. Maybe the pages
of the world flip too quickly or the text
runs backwards, and she is still just
a juvenile, slurring the geometries

of flight, then teetering from limb
　　　　　to limb. Maybe there's no mercy
believable for this age
　　　　　of nuclear fallout and mass extinction,
but reader, believe me:
　　　　　Nature's deus ex machina in the form
of a mature red tail hawk
　　　　　(her mother?) did appear, exploding from the tree-
tops to defend her, scattering
　　　　　the jays like loose change. Who could have foreseen
it? And who could have foreseen
　　　　　another hawk gliding in from the east
as if part of the family?
　　　　　Who could have foreseen daughter
reunited with parents, the rhyme
　　　　　of their bodies a ballast, her hawkness restored?

Returning Home

For Elise

You are the sensation of homeward:
loosening of hands, feet, untightening of back;
the long vowel sounds of rain, ouiseau, moon;

the sudden fluency of a seal slipping
into water. Remember the first time as a child
when—fingers cramping— your fist suddenly slackened

after you wrote your name (your own!)
in a hand curved as if around the stem
of a feather? A deer springs from a clearing

to a copse of trees no man has ever seen.
You: embrace of a black gum tree. And four legs
kneeling down, a body nestling into the long grass.

To the Source

Take my hand: will you bring me to the source,
to the river's mouth? If I rise with the river,
I'll be flooded with cattails and runoff. If I run off

with you, do you know a place beyond the arm
of the state? It's getting late. Lead me to the heart-
land or a body of water, to my earliest language

so we can pledge to soil, seed, and air,
indivisible in a sparrow's first subsong.
What if all's related: the quality of light,

the superfund site, the lump in the breast,
the songbirds sighted too early in spring?
In the smog, the only sunrise that can be seen

stalls out on a TV screen. Perhaps somewhere else
somebody's birthright is sunlight, but in this Big Gulp
country, my body's an artifact of industry: a trial, a test.

PCBs in the bloodstream, exposure to mercury
and lead dioxins. My fertility's uncertain,
and that wheeze you hear could be a symptom,

could be a prickle of grief.
It's getting late and the garden's flooded.
Its dredgings speak of sacrifice: broken teeth

of harrow, patented seeds and chrysanthemum—
engineered blue. When the time comes,
we can count on our kind to reroute the river upstream,

to remake whole cities rather than ourselves. It's getting late,
and the heat's *unseasonable,* but *season,*
which meant once *a proper time, a sowing,*

now means scrounging for another morsel
of land, an ice floe to rest on, or a gesture of hope—
a spell of rain or the essential play of bees

in a force field of strawberries. It's getting late,
the Arctic's burning, and you cannot coax methane
back under permafrost. The mush spits up seal-

skin boots, seeds and microbes,
mammoth bones and pathogens,
viruses that will follow the dotted lines of love.

How does this song go? Is it told in a whisper
with a crack in the voice?
If you tilt your ear to the earth, what do you hear?

It's getting late, and the whales are singing a little flat:
so loud the acoustics of cracking icebergs,
they may be changing their pitch to be heard.

Love Song of the Fig Wasp

—for Amy Savage

The ocean aches for a lush moon.
       I, near- invisible, crave the flowers
inside the fig. That sweetness sings

and swells, pink light calling to my core.
       That solo flight in, all-consumed,
I push and pry inside tight quarters.

Snip! The flesh snags my four-wings,
       takes the pinpoint needles
of my antennae, everything. No matter.

The moon gives and takes away its light.
       The fig too. New-bodied, more ant
than wasp, I creep around the fruit's pips,

bigger than my eyes, make a home
       inside pulp bursting with clusters
and clusters of flowers, ecstasies upon ecstasies!

I lay caches of eggs within the span of that fruit,
       swipe and spread pollen like wallops of jam.
Call it the largesse of pollinators. Call it a future trust.

Yes: I will die locked inside that paradise,
       and my sons, once mated, will too.
But my daughters? They'll carry on what I started;

dressed in pollen, they'll escape, find the next fig.
       Slice it open. You won't find their secrets.
The juice will spill open your lips.

Notes

"Foreign Bodies:" inspired by Chevalier Jackson's Foreign Body Collection at the Mutter Museum and Mary Capello's *Swallow: Foreign Bodies, their Ingestion, Inspiration, and the Curious Doctor who Extracted Them.*

"Field Guide for the 'White' Naturalist:" The identifications are predicated on my readings of Camille Dungy's *Black Nature*: *Four Centuries of African American Nature Poetry,* Herbert C. Covey's *African American Slave Medicine: Herbal and Non-Herbal Treatments* and Robert Hayden's "Middle Passage."

In "Phonics for Grief" and "When the Family No Longer Speaks of their Dead," the notion of language as a shadow comes from Jake Skeets' essay "My Name is Beauty."

"Do I Move You?": The title and part of the first line of the poem reprise Nina Simone's song of the same name.

"Little Edie on Surviving Isolation:" This cento is drawn from the documentaries *Grey Gardens* and *The Beales of Grey Gardens.*

Acknowledgements

I am grateful to the following journals and publications where these poems first appeared, sometimes in slightly different versions.

After Happy Hour Review: "Don't Be Fooled" and "Rock Scramble Haibun"

Anamot Press: "Salt Lick"

Barzakh: "Destroyer of Worlds" and "Hunger"

Bear Review: "On Metaphor as (De-)Composition"

Bellevue Literary Review: "OCD"

The Best of the Net: "Thumbnails of America"

The Briar Cliff Review: "Snowy Owl Nocturne"

Cider Press Review: "Hallelujah" and "The Release"

Cold Mountain Review: "Field Guide for the White Naturalist"; "Ornithology 103"; "Little Edie on Surviving Isolation;" "The Berlin Specimen"

The Dodge: "Whale Fall"

Figure 1: "Vacation in Lyon" and "Fowl at Large"

The Hopper: "Gift of Ammonite"

Kestrel: "In the World of Sham and Nought"

Matter: "Breaking through the Chernobyl Exclusion Zone" and "Pain Bias"

Medmic: "Pneumothorax"

Misfit Magazine: "Tunnel of Silence"

The Offing: "Thumbnails of America"

Painted Bride Quarterly: "Marriage as Hide and Seek"

Permafrost: "Self-Portrait as Barred Owl"

Pleiades: "Taughannock Falls Haibun"

Quarter After Eight: "Diet and Feeding Behavior of the Hagfish, Practicing Witch of the Sea"

Quiddity: "Foreign Bodies"

Santa Clara Review: "Welcome to America"

Spillway: "Self-Portrait as Tomb Raider"

Split Rock Review: "Saltonstall Residency, Ithaca, NY Haibun"

Terrain.org: "To the Source"

Tupelo Quarterly: "Missing Person"

Yes Poetry: "A Small Violence"

Special Thanks

I also wish to thank the Constance Saltonstall Foundation for the Arts, which provided the time and resources to complete several of these poems.

I am deeply grateful for my writing community, and for the conversations, support, and feedback I received from Therese Broderick, Susan Comninos, Jonathan Dubow, Julie Gutmann, jil hanifan, Alyse Knorr, Kayleigh Zaloga, Rae Muhlstock, Kate Partridge, Charlotte Pence, Lucyna Prostko, Courtney Ryan, Christopher Salerno, Amy Savage, Elizabeth Threadgill, and Heather Treseler.

And to the friends who have kept me afloat through these many months of grief, including several mentioned above, as well as Kristin Sorbaro, Erin Cox, Jennifer Clarkson-Greene, Nicole Olivet, Sarah Whipple, Erica Cice, Nan Butterfield, and Kim Wenger. Thank you to my aunts Joan Bunnell and Lisa Vienneau and most especially to my uncle Joe Vienneau. Thank you for listening.

With great appreciation to David Martin for believing in this manuscript.

Thank you to Elise, my partner in crime and ballast in emergency, my love, who has listened to me read new poems over and over again with steadfast support and patience.

And always to my mother, who cultivated my imagination, gifted me with dictionaries and books and a love of making things, who taught me that art, like love, is worth the risk.

About the Author

Sarah Giragosian is the author of the poetry collections *Queer Fish*, a winner of the American Poetry Journal Book Prize (Dream Horse Press, 2017), and *The Death Spiral* (Black Lawrence Press, 2020). In 2023, the University of Akron Press released the craft anthology, *Marbles on the Floor: How to Assemble a Book of Poems*, which she co-edited. Sarah's writing has appeared in such journals as *Orion, Ecotone, Tin House, Pleiades* and *Prairie Schooner*, among others. She teaches at the University at Albany-SUNY.

About the Publisher

Middle Creek Publishing believes that responding to the world through art & literature—and sharing that response—is a vital part of being an artist.

Middle Creek Publishing is a company seeking to make the world a better place through both the means and ends of publishing. We are publishers of quality literature in any genre from authors and artists, both seasoned and those who are undiscovered or under-valued, or under-represented, with a great interest in works which illuminate or embody any aspect of contemplative Human Ecology, defined as the relationship between humans and their natural, social, and built environments.

Middle Creek Publishing's particular interest in Human Ecology is meant to clarify an aspect of the quality in the works we will consider for publication and as a guide to those considering submitting work to us. Our interest is in publishing works which illuminate the human experience through words, story or other content that connects us to each other, our environment, our history, and our potential deeply and more consciously.

Made in United States
North Haven, CT
06 August 2024

55757228R00059